THIS A–Z GUIDE is intended for the general, inquisitive visitor —both as a practical directory of what the area has to offer, and to make available straightforward background information on the unique variety of natural and human history that is here.

The Complete Guide to
Lyme Regis

Italics in the text indicate a

GW00708635

A STREET MAP IS PRINTED ON

Allotments

There are cliff-top allotments above East Cliff, behind the Charmouth Road car park; the sloping land is steadily slipping towards the cliff edge (see *Landslides*). The plots are leased from the Town Council and managed by the local Allotment Association.

Amusement Arcade

Situated above Front Beach on *Marine Parade*, the arcade includes slot machines, interactive video games, and a variety of prize machines.

Mary Anning

Lyme's most famous figure, the fossil-collector Mary Anning was born in 1799, at the time of growing interest in the new popular activity of 'fossiling'. Her father, a carpenter, collected and sold fossil specimens found amongst the rocks of the local cliffs, and her early years spent helping developed into both a lifetime of practical study and a world-wide reputation. In 1811, a year after the death of their father, Mary and her brother Joseph discovered the complete fossilised skeleton of an ichthyosaur, a dolphin-like reptile, in the cliffs east of Lyme. After a careful and lengthy process of removal, the specimen was acquired by the British Museum, and is now in the Natural History Museum, London. Later complete finds include a plesiosaur, a marine reptile, and the first specimen of a pterosaur, a flying dragon-like creature. There is no definitive history of her life, and accounts tend to be sketchy and contradictory, even fictitious, but the Annings were helped from their lowly position through their hard work and endeavour, as well as the financial patronage of sympathetic collectors like Thomas Birch and the Philpot sisters (see *Silver Street*). She died aged forty-eight, and a family headstone marks her burial in the graveyard of the parish church, where there is also a memorial window (see *Churches*). At the *Lyme Regis Museum* there is a display of her life and work including original artefacts and specimens.

Aquarium

See the entry for the *Marine Aquarium*, situated in the warehouses on *The Cobb*.

Art & Craft Galleries

Lyme has a number of galleries showing and selling antique and contemporary pictures, graphic works, objects and crafts. As well as the galleries listed here, there are several open studios selling work directly to the public. A free Gallery Trail leaflet is available from the Tourist Office; also see the entry for *Arts Week*.

Blue Lias Gallery, 47 Coombe Street. 01297 444919
Coombe Street Gallery, 33 Coombe Street. 01297 444817
The Mermaid Shop, The Tudor, Church Street. 01297 443074
The Pelly Gallery, 7 Broad Street. 01297 442760
Town Mill Gallery, Mill Lane. 01297 443579
Tulips Gallery, 10a Broad Street. 01297 445544

Art Materials

The art shop in Broad Street stocks a general range of painting and drawing materials, craft equipment and picture framing.

Fine Art & Framing, 64 Broad Street. 01297 443384
Town Mill Framing, Mill Lane. 01297 444999

Arts Week

The first annual Arts Week was held in 2003. This local event takes place in September and includes open studios, exhibitions, workshops and special activities throughout the town.

Lyme Regis ArtsFest, www.lymeregisartsfest.com

Jane Austen

From the mid eighteenth to early nineteenth centuries the town was a fashionable seaside staging post after taking the waters at

Bath. The Austen family stayed in Lyme Regis in the summer of 1804. Much of her final romantic novel 'Persuasion', written in 1815–16, and published a year after her death in 1818, is set against the backdrop of the town, notably the incident where the character Louisa Musgrove jumped and fell from steps on *The Cobb*. At the end of

Marine Parade, opposite the first buildings on the seaward side, there is a small, elevated Jane Austen Garden, opened in 1975.

Axminster

Situated on the River Axe, five miles north-west of Lyme, the town is famous world-wide for its carpet industry which dates back to 1755. In the early days the Minster bells would be rung when each new carpet was completed. The present firm of Axminster Carpets have a large factory on the southern edge of the town, producing over three-quarters of a million square metres of carpet a year. The street pattern of the old town is medieval, and in part Saxon, centring on the Minster Church and Trinity Square, where a street market is held every Thursday. There is a local museum, and the Arts Café has exhibitions of local art and craft. The London Waterloo–Exeter line, operated by South West Trains, stops at Axminster Station, with a regular bus service providing a link to Lyme Regis (see *Buses*).

Axminster Museum, Church Street. 01297 34137
Arts Café, Old Courthouse, Church Street. 01297 631445

Axmouth & Seaton

Six miles west along the coast, the small seaside town of Seaton sits just beyond the mouth of the River Axe and the ancient port of Axmouth. Situated at the end the Roman Fosse Way, Axmouth was one of the most important trading harbours in the West country up until the fourteenth century, when both cliff falls and

the silting-up of the estuary led to its decline. The mouth of the river has since been deflected eastwards by the spit at the end of the shingle ridge fronting the town, and the village of Axmouth is almost a mile from the sea. The old

concrete river bridge, dating from 1877, is the earliest surviving example in the country and is now used just for pedestrians; and rising above the shingle beach to the west, the series of cliffs round to Beer Head are the western-most chalk outcrops. An electric tramway runs the three miles inland to the attractive town of Colyton along the mudflats of the River Axe, a popular habitat for wading birds (see *Bird Watching*).

Seaton Tramway, Harbour Road. 01297 20375

Bakers

As well as the bakers listed here, fresh bread and cakes, pies and pasties are available from the several *Grocers & Delicatessens*.

Cottage Bakery & Coffee Shop, The Pitt House, off Broad Street. 01297 445515
Town Mill Bakery, Unit 2, Coombe Street. 01297 444035

Banks

Three banks have branches with cash points.

HSBC, 25 Broad Street.
Lloyds, 54 Broad Street.
National Westminster, 22 Broad Street.

Beach Huts

During the summer months the beach huts situated on the *Cart Road*, beneath the western end of *Marine Parade*, are made available by the Town Council for weekly lease (day-use only).

Lyme Regis Town Council, Guildhall Cottage, Church Street. 01297 445175

Beaches

The beach profile along Lyme's coastline is generally of pebble banks at high water, and at lower water gently-sloping sand, with flat exposed limestone ledges beyond. Looking landward, the westernmost beach is *Monmouth Beach*, extending beyond *The Cobb* (there is a small sandy beach at the end of *The Cobb*, beyond the Victoria Pier). Beneath *Marine Parade*, Cobb Gate Beach now has a broader and higher shingle bank as part of the recent coastal protection works, with

the sheltered Front Beach (above) between *The Cobb* harbour and the new jetty replenished and extended with sand imported from Normandy. From Cobb Gate Jetty, *Gun Cliff Beach* fronts the sea defence scheme up to Broad Ledge; then around to Church Cliff and *East Cliff Beach*, and beyond to *Charmouth*. (See *Fossils*, *Rock Pools*, *Swimming*, *Tide Times*).

Bed & Breakfast

There are many guest houses and private homes offering bed and breakfast accommodation in the town, as well as in the surrounding villages and countryside. A current list and booking service is available at the Tourist Information Centre.

Tourist Information Centre, Guildhall Cottage, Church Street. 01297 442138 lyme.tic@westdorset-dc.gov.uk

Bell Cliff

From this elevated vantage point at the bottom of *Broad Street*, it is possible to see a view of *The Cobb* to the west, and the wide panorama of the eastern part of the town and coastline—from the cliffs of *Black Ven*, behind the tower of the parish church, and along much of the coast, taking in *Charmouth*, *Golden Cap*, *Seatown*, West Bay, Chesil Beach and, if clear, the Isle of Portland (see *Jurassic Coast*). Re-named after the alarm bell that once hung here, Bell Cliff was also used as a platform for political

speeches at election times, looking over the original square at the bottom of *Broad Street*. The eighteenth century cannon was originally located at *The Cobb* and suggests the defensive value of this location in Elizabethan times.

Bird Watching

The coast offers opportunities to see many types of sea birds, from the more common residents, such as herring gulls, black-headed gulls, great black-backed gulls and cormorants, shags, gannets and guillemots, to visitors, including various waders, terns, and ocean birds such as fulmars and petrels. *The Undercliff* walk, between Lyme and *Axmouth*, is a densely wooded nature reserve, and home to a wide range of birdlife, including many rarer varieties. Along the *River Lym*, mallard ducks are locals in the town, and further upstream grey wagtails, dippers and kingfishers can be seen; while the estuary of the River Axe, at *Axmouth* and *Seaton*, is a popular feeding ground for many types of wading birds, geese and ducks, with occasional rare visitors. Inland, the hedgerows and woods are busy with songbirds, especially in spring; while buzzards are a common sight wheeling in the skies over higher ground.

Black Ven

The cliffs of Black Ven rise between Lyme and *Charmouth*. 'Ven' is a local word for 'fen', and refers to the boggy slopes of what is Europe's largest coastal landslide. The golden-coloured sandstone and clay layers sit above grey marls and shales that after periods of heavy rain collapse producing rockfalls, slumps and mudflows onto the beach (see strata diagram, below). Up to thirty metres of cliff can be lost in a year of major activity, and in the last decades there has been disruption to the route of the *South West Coast Path* and fairways on the golf course at Timber Hill. Longer ago several routes over the cliffs were completely lost, including the original coast road in the mid-eighteenth century (see *Landslides*).

Blue Plaques

The 700th anniversary of Lyme's Royal Charter, granted in 1284, was celebrated by the installation of metal information plaques on historical buildings and locations throughout the town. A guidebook, 'Signs of

History', to these and other celebratory and informational plaques, linked in a series of four walks, has been published by the Lyme Regis Society.

Boat Building

Boat building at *The Cobb* dates back to the eighteenth-century, and probably long before; from the mid-eighteenth to mid-nineteenth

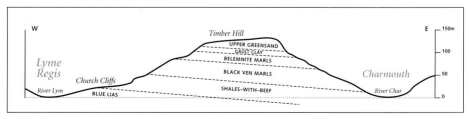

centuries, well over a hundred ships, mainly schooners, were launched from yards here.

Situated west of *The Cobb*, just beyond the *Monmouth Beach* car park, the Boat Building Academy continues the tradition. The building was formerly an outdoor activity centre, re-opening in 1997 with refurbished workshops and facilities. The present-day school runs professional thirty-eight week courses in traditional and modern boat building techniques, as well as shorter wfive-day and weekend courses.

Boat Building Academy, Monmouth Beach. 01297 445545 www.boatbuildingacademy.com

Boat Trips

A number of boats at *The Cobb* operate regular fishing trips in *Lyme Bay*, and also sight-seeing trips along the coast (see *Fishing, Sea*). Dates and times of departure and other details are announced on boards along the quayside opposite the *Lifeboat Station*.

Bookshops

Lyme has one bookseller of general new books: Serendip Books in *Broad Street*; and several dealers in second-hand books—these can also be found in collectors' and charity shops. Publications on local subjects are also available from museum and specialist shops (see entries for *Museums* and *Fossil Shops*). Chimp & Zee, is dedicated to the children's books and work of Catherine and Laurence Anholt.

The Bookshop, The Old Bonded Store, Marine Parade. 01297 444820
Chimp & Zee, Bookshop by the Sea, 51 Broad Street. 01297 442233
The Sanctuary Bookshop, 65 Broad Street. 01297 445815
Serendip Books, 11 Broad Street. 01297 442594

Bowls

The bowling green and clubhouse are situated at the end of Ozone Terrace, by the *Monmouth Beach* car park, and run by Lyme Regis Bowling Club (see *Clubs & Societies*).

Bridport

Eight miles east of Lyme and a mile inland from West Bay (or Bridport Harbour), this former port is now a busy town with a wide selection of shops, public houses and restaurants. Its wealth originally grew from the rope and net manufacturing industry, which dates back to the early medieval period. The raw material, hemp, had been grown in the surrounding country since Roman times. The wide streets and walks once

used for the twisting and drying of the fibres remain, along with examples of the solidly built rope-works. The three main streets, East, West and South Streets, meet at the arcaded eighteenth-century Town Hall, and are lined with many fine Georgian and Victorian buildings. Of particular interest are the Quaker Meeting House and The Chantry—a medieval lighthouse, both in South Street. There is an excellent local museum; and the Arts Centre has a lively programme of art and craft exhibitions, theatrical productions, concerts, events and workshops. A street market is held on Wednesdays, and on Saturdays antique and collector's stalls extend along South Street.

Bridport Arts Centre, South Street. 01308 424204
Bridport Museum, South Street. 01308 422116

Broad Street

Originally named simply West Street, Lyme Regis's main shopping street descends from the junction of *Pound Street* and *Silver Street* at the top of town to Bridge Street at the bottom.

There is a variety of shops and restaurants in Broad Street, and two of Lyme's most well-known buildings face each other diagonally across the street: the Royal Lion Hotel, and the sadly unused and neglected Three Cups, closed in 1991 (see *Hotels*). Several of the notable

buildings have explanatory plaques. With Lyme's rise in popularity, many were modernised during the late eighteenth and early nineteenth centuries, the new more fashionable Georgian façades hiding considerably earlier building. Towards the bottom of the hill, on the western side, the pavement and buildings rise above the level of the road, which was formerly known as Cornhill. In front was the site of the Shambles market-place, destroyed along with several buildings at this end of the town by the fire of 1844. From here the elevated buildings on *Bell Cliff* interrupt the wide view of the coastline to the east. At the foot of the hill was the original town square, behind *Cobb Gate* (now the car park), the point of entry until 1800 for all goods landed at *The Cobb*. The custom-house, which dated back to Elizabethan times (on the site of the public toilets), and the original Three Cups, were both lost in the 1844 fire.

Buddle Bridge

Best viewed looking back from *Gun Cliff Walk*, or from the beach below, the final bridge over

the *River Lym* has been adapted many times. Some of the original fourteenth-century medieval masonry still forms part of the bridge, and parts have been found

in basements of adjacent buildings. 'Buddle' means 'narrow or enclosed passage', and for centuries would have been the channel for the town's sewage before it entered the sea—or the beach if low-tide. Bridge Street, between *Broad Street* and *Church Street*, was widened for motor traffic in 1913, and buildings that stood on and alongside the bridge were demolished, including The Fossil Depot—which sold both fresh fish and fossil specimens.

Buses

The principal daily bus service is the 31, connecting Taunton, Ilminster, Chard, *Axminster*, *Uplyme*, Lyme Regis, *Charmouth*, *Morecombelake*, Chideock, *Bridport*, Dorchester and Weymouth. Buses are hourly Monday to Saturday, and two-hourly on Sundays. The X53/X54 is a daily service connecting (in summary) Exeter, *Seaton*, Lyme Regis, *Bridport*, Weymouth and Wareham; the service is about every two hours. The 899 connects Lyme Regis, *Rousdon*, *Axmouth*, *Seaton*, Colyford, Beer, Branscombe, Sidford, Sidmouth, Newton Poppleford, Budleigh Salterton and Exmouth; it runs about every two hours, with no service at weekends. It should be noted that heading east, buses stop outside the *Post Office* at the top of *Broad Street*; heading west, at the bus shelter by the *Cobb Gate* car park at the bottom of the hill.

Butchers

Lyme's last remaining butcher, Pattimores of Coombe Street closed in 2007. The clothing shop, Hilary Highet, at the top of Broad Street still has the typically tiled interior of its former occupant carefully preserved. Butchers selling quality local meat can be found in *Axminster*, *Bridport* and *Charmouth*; also see *Grocers & Delicatessens*.

Cafés & Tea Rooms

Lyme has a good choice of cafés serving food and refreshments during the day; as well as those listed here, many *Restaurants* and *Hotels* open for morning coffee, lunches and afternoon cream teas.

Bell Cliff Restaurant, 5–6 Broad Street. 01297 442459
Beach House Café, 24 Marine Parade. 01297 445923

Bubble & Squeak Café, Cobb Road. 01297 444676

Café Sol, 1a Coombe Street. 01297 443404

Coffee Shop & Tea Room. Old Bonded Store, Marine Parade.

Cottage Bakery & Coffee Shop, The Pitt House,
off Broad Street. 01297 445515

Country Stocks, 53 Broad Street. 01297 442961

The Fudge and Coffee House, 9 Broad Street.

Jalito's, 14 Broad Street. 01297 445008

Janes Café, 29 Marine Parade. 01297 442331

The Old Boathouse, Marine Parade. 01297 445702

Town Mill Bakery, Unit 2, Coombe Street. 01297 444035

Camping & Caravans

There are a number of excellent locations for camping and caravaning in the surrounding area. The level of amenities provided vary from one site to another—brochures and further information are available on request.

Hook Farm Camping & Caravaning Park, Gore Lane, Uplyme. 01297 442801

Manor Farm Holiday Centre, The Street, Charmouth. 01297 560226

Monkton Wyld Farm Caravan Park, Monkton Wyld, Charmouth. 01297 34525

Newlands Holidays, Charmouth. 01297 560259

Seadown Caravan Park, Bridge Road, Charmouth. 01297 560154

Shrubbery Touring Park, Rousdon. 01297 442227

Wood Farm Caravan Park, Axminster Road, Charmouth. 01297 560697

Cannington Viaduct

Built for the Axminster–Lyme Regis branch line, which operated from 1903 to 1965 (see *Railways*), this huge concrete construction spans a quiet valley south of Holcombe, just off the westerly coast road. Nearly two hundred metres long and almost a thirty metres high, its ten massive arches were built without scaffolding, the concrete being

conveyed by aerial cables and poured directly into formwork. Crushed flint was used in the concrete aggregate, excavated from nearby chalk cuttings on the line.

Car Boot Sales

Held on Sundays from May to October, the nearest regular sales are at Raymond's Hill, off the A35 near *Axminster*, from early morning; and from mid morning at Combpyne Hill, near Rousdon (see entry for *Combpyne & Rousdon*).

Car Parking

Lyme's steep and relatively narrow streets were not made for large vehicles, or for the heavy traffic of the summer months. There is some restricted on-street parking in *Broad Street*, and *Silver Street*; and the town has a choice of several car parks (see the *Street Map*, inside back cover). There are long-stay car parks on Charmouth Road on the eastern side of the town; Holmbush at the top of *Cobb Road* on the western side; and Hill Road in the centre of the town. Short-stay car parks, usually very busy in summer, are situated at *Monmouth Beach*; off *Broad Street*; and *Cobb Gate*. Seasonal park and ride services operate a few miles out of town—on the west, from Sidmouth Road to Cobb Square; and on the east, from Charmouth Road to the town.

Cart Road

The original route for the passage of goods landed by boat at Lyme Regis, from *The Cobb* and beside the beach to *Cobb Gate* and the town. As part of the latest coastal protection scheme and the building of a new outer sea wall, the road has now

been extended around the buildings on the seaward side at the western end of *Marine Parade* to make a promenade-style walkway between the town and *The Cobb* harbour.

Charmouth

The main street of Lyme's easterly neighbour, with its elegant Georgian villas, is set back several hundred metres inland. The settlement dates back to Saxon times, and it is recorded that an invasion attempt by thirty-five Danish ships took place in AD 833. The sixteenth-century Queen's Arms Hotel is the oldest building and Charles II secretly stayed the night here after fleeing, following his defeat by Cromwell at Worcester. Linked by a wooden footbridge, the beaches either side of the mouth of the River Char are rich in fossils, although

the cliffs are dangerous and should be approached with caution, particularly after heavy rain. The Heritage Coast Centre (once a cement-mill) on the seafront displays fossils and geological specimens and information about the natural history of the *Jurassic Coast*, and the shop below hires geology hammers for fossil-hunting. It should be noted that it is only possible to walk the beach route between Lyme and Charmouth at low tide. See *Black Ven*, *Fossils*, *Tide-times*.

Charmouth Heritage Coast Centre, Lower Sea Lane. 01297 560772 www.charmouth.org

Chemists

There is a dispensing chemist in the town and at the group practice on the road to *Uplyme*.

Boots the Chemist, 45 Broad Street. 01297 442026
Lloyds Pharmacy, Lyme Regis Community Care Centre, Uplyme Road. 01297 442981

Church Street

At right angles to Bridge Street, the lower part of Church Street was originally the Butter Market. Here stands one of Lyme's earliest

surviving buildings, the former Tudor House Hotel (now a gallery), built in the latter part of the sixteenth century, although the frontage is Georgian—

many of Lyme's older buildings, particularly in *Broad Street*, were built earlier than their present appearances would suggest. Opposite is a passage, Long Entry, which once led on to the path across the cliffs to *Charmouth*; the route collapsed in a landslide around 1750. The parish church of St Michael, opposite *Monmouth Street*, dates back to Norman times (see *Churches*), while on the corner the present Old Monmouth Hotel was formerly an inn, the Golden Hart. Beyond, Church Street becomes the Charmouth Road and continues up and along the valley side to Timber Hill and the *South West Coast Path*.

Churches

The parish church of St Michael (illustrated) is on the east side of *Church Street*, with coastal views from the tower and the rear of the graveyard. It largely dates from the early sixteenth century, although there is evidence of Norman building —it is recorded

that a there was a church in Lyme in 1145, the settlement in those days probably centring on the bottom of *Church Street*. The nineteenth century Roman Catholic church of St Michael and St George in *Silver Street* provided a place of worship for many of the new incomers and visitors to the town. The natives of Lyme being, like those of many West country towns, traditionally Protestant and non-conformist, and their needs in turn were provided by the Baptist Chapel at the top of *Sherborne Lane*, and what was then the Congregationalist Chapel in *Coombe Street*—this building (dating from 1755) now houses the *Dinosaurland* museum. Another former chapel is at 33 *Sherborne Lane*, a Methodist place of worship in the first half of the nineteenth century.

Church of St Michael and St George, Silver Street.
Lyme Regis Baptist Church, 2 Sherborne Lane.
Parish Church of St Michael, Church Street.

Cinema

With a resident population of around three thousand Lyme Regis is the smallest town in the country to have its own cinema. Opened

in 1937, the privately-run Regent is a period piece from the days long before the multiplex. It presents a weekly programme of general releases, as well as hosting the Lyme Regis Film Society's out-of-season subscription programme (see *Clubs & Societies*).

Regent Cinema, Broad Street. 01297 442053

Clothing

There are several outlets in Lyme for clothes designed and made locally: at the top of *Broad Street*, Hilary Highet sells her knitwear designs; opposite, the milliner Pop Goes the Weasel sells bespoke hats, and accessories. In *Silver Street*, Sublyme sells vintage clothing; and La-Di-Da bespoke bridal wear. Outdoor clothes and leisurewear are stocked by Lyme Bay Clothing and Lyme Leisure; and watersport and fashion brands by Lyme Bay Surf. Fuego, in *Coombe Street*, sells a range of garments and accessories imported from South America.

Calico Boutique, Cobb Square. 01297 444484
Casual Wear, Old Bonded Store, Marine Parade. 01297 444829

Focus, 62 Broad Street. 01297 443565
Fuego, 5a Coombe Street. 01297 443933
Hilary Highet, 35 Broad Street. 01297 443824
Hilary Highet Studio, 63a Silver Street. 01297 443454
La-Di-Da, 40 Silver Street, 01297 445700
Lyme Bay Clothing, 20 Broad Street. 01297 445198
Lyme Bay Surf, 27 Broad Street. 01297 444407
Lyme Leisure, 30 Broad Street. 01297 445030
Persuasion, 19 Marine Parade. 01297 445291
Pop Goes the Weasel, 32a Broad Street. 01297 443393
Primary Colours, 50 Broad Street. 01297 445655
Sublyme, 5 Silver Street. 01297 444397

Clubs & Societies

A current list of local organisations, with contact names and telephone numbers, is available from the Town Council offices.

Lyme Regis Town Council, Guildhall Cottage, Church Street. 01297 445175

Elinor Coade

Born into a wealthy Lyme family, and owner of the then recently built Belmont House on *Pound Street* from 1784 until her death in 1821, Elinor Coade gained fame and success as a manufacturer. She set up a London factory in Lambeth in the late 1760s for the manufacture of Coade stone, an extremely resilient composite material that could be moulded to make fireplaces, statuary and architectural ornaments. The unique formula consisted of finely ground flint, sand, glass and clay—formed and kiln-fired at a high temperature for several days. Although the material was expensive, its resemblance to natural stone ensured that it proved very popular, and many buildings in London are still decorated with products from the factory, as is Belmont (for almost forty years the residence of the author *John Fowles*). The ammonite paving

outside the entrance to the *Lyme Regis Museum* is of recent Coade stone, and there are other examples inside the museum.

Coastguard

The Lyme Regis Coastguard office, formerly at the bottom of *Cobb Road*, is presently in the ex-telephone exhange on Sidmouth Road, and is responsible for the twelve mile stretch of coast from *Seatown* in the east, to *Axmouth* harbour in the west. Emergency 999 calls are directed to the district call centre at Portland, who in turn will alert the local coastguard.

The Cobb

Functioning both as a harbour and a breakwater, protecting the town from the worst of the channel storms, the Cobb was originally constructed from oak piles driven into the seabed and infilled with boulders. It probably dates back to as early as the thirteenth century; records from the 1370s describe much damage to the town and shipping in great storms, and the complete destruction of the Cobb. The structure was repaired and refined over the following centuries with trade and fishing flourishing in and out of the sheltered haven and boatyards launching new vessels. (See entries on *Boat Building*; *Fishing, Sea*; *Lyme Bay* and *Smuggling*.) Until the middle of the eighteenth century the sea at high tide cut off the Cobb from the land—the onshore

wave action replenished the protective shingle banks on the easterly beaches and scoured the sand from the harbour floor. Much of what we see of the Cobb today was built in the late eighteenth and nineteenth centuries, using massive blocks of Portland stone. The Southern Arm, extending beyond the enclosed

harbour dates from the 1790s; the High Wall was constructed in 1819–20, and further strengthened following damage from heavy storms in 1824; the Victoria Pier and North Wall date from the 1840s; and the causeway beneath

the High Wall and alongside the harbour from the 1850s. Nowadays, the Cobb is classified and protected as a Grade 1 listed building. The coastal protection work carried out between 2005 and 2007 extended the Southern Arm rock defence, improving the sheltering effect of the breakwater; the rock armour at the beach end of the North Wall was re-aligned; and sand that had built up in the harbour moved along to the Front Beach. Situated by the slipway to the harbour is the RNLI *Lifeboat Station*, providing a rescue service for a wide sector of the waters of *Lyme Bay*, while the Cobb is managed from the Harbourmaster's Office next door. On Victoria Pier, part of the warehouse buildings house the *Marine Aquarium* which as well as its specimen tanks has displays about the history of this unique structure.

Harbourmaster's Office, The Cobb. 01297 442137

Cobb Gate

Nowadays the area at the bottom of *Broad Street* taken up by the small car park with its millennial clock gives little indication of its former purpose. Until the end of the eighteenth century, all goods landed

at *The Cobb* had to be brought nearly half a

mile along the foreshore *Cart Road* to this busy point, with its warehouses, customs-house and fish market. The Assembly Rooms replaced the warehouses in the 1770s, as a fashionable meeting place for the rising numbers of wealthy visitors. In turn the building became a social club and then a cinema, eventually being demolished in 1928.

Cobb Road

Because goods landed at *The Cobb* had to be cleared through *Cobb Gate* in the town, Cobb Road only made the full ascent to *Pound Street* in the first half of the nineteenth century. The old route between this part of the town and *The Cobb* was along Stile Lane, and through what is now Lister Gardens (illustrated). In 1962 there was major subsidence to the land and the road in this area following a landslide in *Langmoor*

Gardens. On the west side at the top, behind the Holmbush car park, the footpath leads to Ware Cliffs (see *Ware*) and *The Undercliff* walk. By the entrance to Lister Gardens there is a stone plaque marking the '*John Fowles* Path' that continues on the east side down to *The Cobb*. Towards the bottom of the steepest part of the hill, on the right, are the old coastguard cottages of Cobb Terrace, and further down, at harbour level, opposite where the end of *Marine Parade* joins Cobb Square, is the evocatively named Ozone Terrace. Built on the site of a former boatyard, the name of this terrace of Victorian houses suggesting the change in the town's prime activity from working harbour to coastal resort.

Combpyne & Rousdon

Rousdon is situated on the coast road west to *Axmouth* and *Seaton*. Much of the village was built in the 1870s to house the workers on the new estate and house built by the Peek family, whose wealth was amassed from the

tea trade. Rousdon Mansion was built in an unusual timbered Flemish-Tudor style, with southerly views to extensive gardens and the sea. The estate was sold in 1938 and became the home of Allhallows School until 1999, when it

was sold off piecemeal for housing; a public bridleway passes through the grounds in front of the main house. Just under a mile inland, in a deep valley, is the picturesque hamlet of Combpyne, with its twelfth-century church and its pond—known locally as 'The Harbour'. From May to October there is a popular Sunday morning car boot sale at Combpyne Hill; directions are given from the coast road.

Coombe Street

Winding back from Bridge Street beside the river, along the foot of the valley—or coombe, this was Lyme's main street in medieval times. It would have been lined with a mixture of buildings: inns, merchant's houses, working-class dwellings such as seamen's and weavers' cottages; at the far end was Mill Green, much of which was destroyed by fire in 1803, including its cloth mill. As noted in the entry for *Public Houses*, there were

eight pubs in Coombe Street at the beginning of the twentieth century—now just the Ship remains, by Mill Lane, and the Angel at Mill Green. For years the main inn was the George, by the side of which ran the small passage through to *George's Square*; in front would have a been a small market square. The imposing Congregationalist chapel, built in 1755, now houses the *Dinosaurland* museum. Opposite

Monmouth Street is Mill Lane, which goes down to the *Town Mill*, a renovated and working watermill.

Thomas Coram

Born in *Coombe Street* in the late 1660s of a seafaring family, this wealthy merchant and generous philanthropist made a fortune trading with the American Colonies, eventually returning to England in 1720. Affected by the plight of the many illegitimate and abandoned children in London, he worked tirelessly to establish and finance the famous Foundling Hospital, Bloomsbury, which opened in the 1740s to feed, clothe and educate. His fortune gone, he died in 1751, having been made a Freeman of the Borough of Lyme Regis in 1749. Coram Court and the solidly Gothic Coram Towers at the corner of Pound Road and *Pound Street* are named in his honour, and there is a stained glass window dedicated to his memory in St Michael's parish church (see *Churches*).

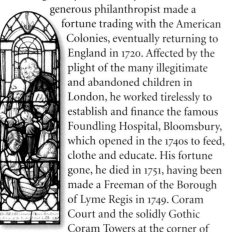

Cricket

The topography of Lyme Regis's location doesn't provide much level cricket-pitch-size land—the Uplyme & Lyme Regis Cricket Club team playing regular competitive league cricket at King George's Field, *Uplyme* (see *Clubs & Societies*).

Cycling

The country in all directions around Lyme Regis is excellent for cycling. In a westerly direction towards the valley of the River Axe, and along the coastline, the country is quite open with elevated roads, the lanes following the combes and valleys; while to the east and the north the country is more undulating, the roads winding, and up and down. The Blackdown Hills, north of *Axminster,* the *Marshwood Vale*, north of *Charmouth*, the entire area from the River Axe to the River Brit at *Bridport*—over a hundred square miles—is perfect for exploring by cycle. The Ordnance Survey 1:25 000 Lyme Regis & Bridport sheet (Explorer 116) is the best guide for an overview of the landscape, and its network of roads, lanes and bridleways. The National Cycle Network Route 2 links the 30 miles between Dorchester, the county town, and Lyme Regis.

Dentists

All of Lyme's dental practices have an emergency service.

Kent House Dental Care, Silver Street. 01297 443442
Lyme Bay Dentistry, 63 Broad Street. 01297 442907
M R Symes, 41 Silver Street. 01297 442846

Dinosaurland

Housed in an eighteenth century former chapel, this museum has a comprehensive display of local fossils, geological specimens, skeletons, and models of dinosaurs. The museum is open daily and guided fossil-hunting walks are organised regularly throughout the year;

and there is a well-stocked shop selling fossils, minerals and publications.

Dinosaurland, Coombe Street. 01297 443541
www.dinosaurland.co.uk

Diving

Many local and visiting clubs dive regularly in *Lyme Bay*, either with their own inflatable rigs, or chartering boats from *The Cobb*. As well as the attractions of reef diving in the clear waters, there are several historic shipwrecks—notably the 'Bay Gitano', a 3000-ton steamship sunk in 1918, just one and a half miles offshore, and the 'Rotorua', a 110-ton liner sunk in 1917, twenty-five miles out from Lyme. Most of the diving clubs and charter boats post information on their websites—search for 'Diving in Lyme Bay'.

Doctors

The group practice on the road to *Uplyme* has a casualty department (see also *Hospitals*).

Kent House Health Centre, Silver Street. 01297 443399
Lyme Regis Community Care Centre, Uplyme Road. 01297 445777

Dogs

The exercising of dogs is completely banned from most of the beaches from 1st May to 30th September, exceptions being *Monmouth Beach* and *East Cliff Beach*. Throughout the town dogs should be kept on a lead, and naturally anything deposited must be removed and disposed of by the owner. Dog wardens are employed by the District and Town Councils, with the power to impose fines.

East Cliff Beach

Beyond *Gun Cliff Beach* and the promontory of Broad Ledge, the beach beneath Church Cliff, The Spittles and *Black Ven* extends beyond to *Charmouth*. Above, the land has a long history of instability, and there has been significant recent land-slipping and mudslides onto the beach, particularly following periods of heavy rain. The displacing of rock makes the beach popular for fossil-hunting, and over the years some of Lyme's most important finds have

come from the Blue Lias here (see *Mary Anning*, *Fossils*, and *Landslides*). The strange phenomenon of a spontaneous fire occured beneath Church Cliff in 1908, when a mound of fallen oil-shales burned for several months—the 'Lyme Volcano' and its sulphurous smoke became a popular tourist attraction.

Fireworks

Firework displays organised to raise funds for local charities are held several times a year from the North Wall at *The Cobb*. The biggest display is the annual Guy Fawkes celebration, held on the evening of the nearest Saturday to 5th November, and follows a torch-light procession and the lighting of a bonfire on the harbour beach.

Fish & Chip Shops

As would be expected of a seaside town, there are several take-away fish and chip shops, as well as kiosks along *Marine Parade* and by *The Cobb* beach during the summer months.

Cobb Gate Fish Bar, Cobb Gate.
Janes Café, 29 Marine Parade. 01297 442331
Lyme Fish Bar, 34 Coombe Street. 01297 442375

Fishing, Coarse & Game

Established for thirty years, Amherst Lodge Fly Fishery, situated just past *Uplyme*, has four acres of freshwater trout lakes fed by the *River Lym*; while Lower Bruckland Farm, just north of the *Axmouth*/Musbury junction on the A3052 has three fishing lakes stocked with rainbow and brown trout. Wood Farm at *Charmouth* has two lakes totalling around an acre, stocked with carp, rudd, roach, tench and perch. Details of fishing further afield is available on the website run by The Tackle Box (see *Fishing Tackle*), and information about fishing

on the River Axe, along with current reports, is posted on the dedicated website run by the Kersbrook Hotel in Lyme Regis.

Amherst Lodge, St Mary's Lane, Yawl. 01297 442773
Lower Bruckland Farm, Musbury. 01297 551197
Wood Farm, Charmouth. 01297 560697
www.riveraxe.co.uk

Fishing, Sea

As befits a coastal settlement, fishing was Lyme's original main activity (along with salt production in Saxon times), reaching its heyday in the nineteenth century, with some of the county's largest trawlers moored at *The Cobb*. Nowadays, there are around twenty or more boats involved in commercial activities, ranging from deep sea trawling and harvesting shellfish, to running seasonal fishing trips in *Lyme Bay*. Times of departure of charter boats, and other details are announced on boards on the quayside opposite the *Lifeboat Station*—some of the mackerel and deep sea fishing boats are: Amaretto III, Blue Turtle, Frances Jane, Jozilee, Kraken, Marie F, Neptune, Pegasus, Sunbeam, and Susie B (images and descriptions, along with contact details are available on The Tackle Box's website below). Species of fish that can be caught include bass, bream, cod, conger eel, dabs, huss, mackerel, mullet, plaice, pollack, ray, skate, sole and whiting; and living specimens of many of these can be seen at the *Marine Aquarium* on *The Cobb*. Shore fishing with rod and line for flat fish is excellent along the beaches and ledges (see *Beaches*). Regular contests for both shore and deep sea fishing are organised by the Lyme Regis Sea Angling Club (See *Clubs & Societies*).

Fishing Tackle

The shop at *The Cobb* stocks a wide range of sea, coarse and game fishing tackle, as well as fresh, live and frozen baits. The excellent website offers a wide range of expert information and advice about both sea and freshwater fishing in the area.

The Tackle Box, 20 Marine Parade. 01297 443373
www.tackleboxlymeregis.co.uk.

Fishmongers

The former Coastguard watch-house (see *Smuggling*), at *The Cobb* end of *Marine Parade*, has sold fish since 1934. It sells a selection of seasonal fresh fish, as well as local *Lyme Bay* shellfish—crabs, lobster and shrimps.

Wet Fish Shop, Cobb Square. 01297 444205

Football

Lyme Regis Football Club, 'The Seasiders' founded in 1885, play regularly in the Perry Street League. The team's ground was formerly on the west side of the town on Sidmouth Road—an exposed playing field with a 1930s stand seating two hundred spectators. The timber structure was destroyed in a storm in 1970 and a move was made to the present ground on allotment land at Davey Fort, above East Cliff and overlooking *Lyme Bay*. Despite plans to build a new stand, a clubhouse and dugout are the only facilities. The pitch is increasingly threatened by land slippage and the proposed next phase of coastal protection works

on the eastern side of Lyme Regis is intended to stabilise the site. (see *Clubs & Societies*).

Fossil Shops

The fossil shops of Lyme Regis continue a local trade that began in the late eighteenth century, with the influx of fossil-hunters and devotees of the new science of palaeontology. *Mary Anning*'s father had collected and sold specimens as curiosities to visitors, and today the supply of much of the stock still depends on the skilful removal and preparation of local finds.

Langdons Originals, The Old Bonded Store, Marine Parade. 01297 552044
Mike's Minerals & Fossils, 7 Drakes Way. 01297 444405
The Lyme Fossil Shop, 4 Bridge Street. 01297 442088
The Old Forge Fossil Shop, 15 Broad Street. 01297 445977

Fossils

Lyme Regis has been famous since the late eighteenth century for its Liassic fossils, when the study of these remains of ancient plants and creatures became a popular new science, although its fossil wealth had been noted in 1673 by the natural philosopher John Ray. The fossils found on the beaches, and in the rocks of the cliffs along the coastline, are the remains of the marine life of the seas that covered the land during Jurassic times (see *Geology*). The most common finds are ammonites, spiral-

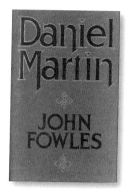

shelled molluscs; belemnites, bullet-shaped squid-like creatures; and various bivalved molluscs such as gryphaea. Lyme has famously turned up rarer and larger finds, such as ichthyosaurs and plesiosaurs, both large marine reptiles (see *Mary Anning*—Lyme's most famous fossil-hunter). The best beaches are *Monmouth Beach*, particularly for ammonites; and *East Cliff Beach* between Lyme and Charmouth; and the best times of year are spring and autumn when the high-tides wash away at the base of the cliffs. It should always be remembered that the cliffs are extremely dangerous, and that safe fossil-hunting is done away from the rock-faces amongst the fallen rocks that litter the beach. Regular guided excursions are organised by both *Dinosaurland* and the *Lyme Regis Museum*, and there are several *Fossil Shops* selling specimens, equipment and publications. The highly successful annual Fossil Festival takes place over three days in May (event postponed for 2008), centred around the *Lyme Regis Museum* and *The Guildhall*; and a wide range of activites include talks, displays, field trips as well as visiting experts from the Natural History Museum, London.

John Fowles

Resident in Lyme from the 1960s until his death in 2005, this world famous author was actively involved in the preservation and interpretation of the town. From 1978 until 1988 he was Honorary Curator of the *Lyme Regis Museum*, and wrote several studies on aspects of local history, including 'A Short History of Lyme Regis'. His many novels include 'The Collector' (1963), 'The Magus' (1966), 'Daniel Martin' (1977) and famously 'The French Lieutenant's Woman' (1969) which was filmed in 1980 on location in 'Victorian-costume' Lyme Regis, directed by Karel Reisz, and starring Meryl Streep and Jeremy Irons. Serendip Books in *Broad Street* has kept its period signage 'C. Chapman, bookseller' from the filming, while the *Lyme Regis Museum* has a display of publications, photographs and original material by the author.

Garages

The nearest petrol stations are in *Uplyme* and at *Rousdon* on the A3052 *Seaton* road.

Rousdon Garage, Rousdon. 01297 442228
Uplyme Services, Lyme Road, Uplyme. 01297 444650

Geology

The geology of the Lyme's site and coastline consists of rocks formed during the Jurassic period—which ended 140 million years ago. During this period, of between 30 and 45 million years, what is now the British Isles was largely covered by a shallow sea, fed by rivers carrying sediment from higher land. It is the residue of the creatures that inhabited these seas, along with the clays and sand that were laid down on the seabed, that make up the rocks of the present-day cliffs and shoreline. The town is partly built on and surrounded by layers of unstable rock; these are adversely affected by periods of heavy rain, resulting in erosion and landslides—this single factor has restrained the town's coastal growth. (See *Jurassic Coast, Landslides* and *Fossils*.) The web pages by Dr Ian West of the School of Ocean and Earth Science, University of Southampton are highly recommended, and present detailed field studies and descriptions of the geology of the entire Wessex Coast, well illustrated with photographs, maps and diagrams.

www.soton.ac.uk/~imw/index.htm

George's Square

Just off *Monmouth Street*, this small square can also be approached through a passage (or drangway, 'drang'means 'narrow') on *Coombe Street*. It was once occupied by the George, the town's largest and most important inn up until the middle of the eighteenth century. The square, to the rear of the inn, would probably have consisted of both stables and a loading yard for packhorses, as well as a market area.

The George was lost in the disastrous fire of 1844, which destroyed forty houses and six inns along *Coombe Street* and behind to *Broad Street*. Today, the square (in fact now a triangle) is a memorial garden, enclosed in 1908.

Golden Cap

The most visible landmark on the easterly coastline around from Lyme Regis, this sandstone-capped cliff is the highest point on the south coast of England, at 191 metres (or 618 feet) above sea-level. The seven formations of geological strata rise from Liassic clay and sands at the foot to Gault Clay and finally a resistant top layer of Upper Greensand—the iron content has oxidised to produce the distinctive golden colouration.

Golf

There are two courses nearby open to non-members. Lyme Regis Golf Club, founded in 1893, is situated on the road to *Charmouth*; it has 18-holes over a 6,000 yard distance, and impressive views of *Lyme Bay*. Westerly along the coast there is another cliff-top course at *Axmouth*. Mini-golf can be played at Lister Gardens, at the top of *Langmoor Gardens*.

Axecliff Golf Club, Axmouth, Seaton. 01297 24371
Lyme Regis Golf Club, Timber Hill. 01297 442963

Greengrocers

Lyme Regis now has just one greengrocer and fruiterer (see *Grocers & Delicatessens* below).

Cauli & Flowers, 49 Broad Street. 01297 443192

Grocers & Delicatessens

All three shops stock a wide range of provisions, including dairy, meats, pastries, preserves, cakes and confectionery; the Co-operative supermarket stocks a full range of grocery, household and licensed products. Collins sells a variety of wholefood and organic products including fruit and vegetables.

Collins, 21 Broad Street. 01297 442076
Co-operative, 38 Broad Street. 01297 442082
Jalito's, 14 Broad Street. 01297 445008

Guest Houses

See *Bed & Breakfast*.

Guided Tours

Several organised tours of the town and beaches are available during the summer months. Fossil-hunting walks are organised year-round by *Dinosaurland* and the *Lyme Regis Museum*; in addition, aspects of the town, such as its ghosts and historical conflicts also have regular tours, starting from *The Guildhall*. Information on all guided tours are available from the Tourist Information Centre. A good, albeit silent, companion to interpreting the history of the town through its streets and buildings is to be found in John Fowles' small guidebook *Three Town Walks*.

Tourist Information Centre, Guildhall Cottage, Church Street. 01297 442138 lyme.tic@westdorset-dc.gov.uk

The Guildhall

The Guildhall—the town hall of a town granted a royal charter (Lyme's right to a merchant's guild was granted in 1284)—has stood on this

site, by the corner of *Church Street* and Bridge Street, for over four hundred years. The last restoration was Victorian, although the building dates back to the 1600s; the closed-in space of the ground floor, now occupied by the Town Council offices, was the arched fish market. The court chamber was on the first floor, and the stocks and jail building would have been in the area between the Guildhall and the *Lyme Regis Museum*—named the 'Cockmoil', an old dialect term for prison.

Gun Cliff Beach

Apart from at low tide, the beach beneath *Gun Cliff Walk* now almost wholly consists of massive rock armour installed in the 1990s sea-defence scheme. The *River Lym* flows into the sea

here, and there are views back upstream beneath the walk-way and *Buddle Bridge*. Along to the eastern end of the beach the rocks give way to sand, and at low tide the Liassic limestone ledges of Long Ledge and Broad Ledge are exposed up to two hundred metres offshore. Much stone was removed from these ledges during the nineteenth century by sea-quarrying for construction material, and as a consequence the problem of coastal erosion was increased.

Gun Cliff Walk

Gun Cliff was so-named bcause it was here that the town's battery of defensive cannon were kept from Elizabethan times. Extending east from the small

car park at *Cobb Gate*, the meandering walkway is now part of an extensive construction scheme completed in 1995. The development integrates new sea-defences, the old and new sea walls between *Cobb Gate* and Church Cliffs, while also subtly housing a sewage treatment plant, evident by the ventilation tower in front of the *Marine Theatre*, and the huge double doors beneath that give access to the works.

Hair & Beauty

Paul's is a men's barbershop; In the Pink is a beauty salon, while the others are both women's and men's hairdressers.

Danni's 2, Unit 3 Coombe Street. 01297 445223
In the Pink, 59 Silver Street. 01297 444880
Making Waves, 53 Silver Street. 01297 442918
Paul's Hairdressers, 67a Broad Street. 01297 442442
Style Inn Hair Salon, 5 Drakes Way. 01297 442750

Horse Riding

Four miles north of Lyme, Higher Pound Riding Centre offers instruction for all ages and abilities, including jumping, on a range of horses, as well as hacking in the nearby woods.

Higher Pound Riding Centre, Monkton Wyld.
01297 678747

Hospitals

The nearest hospitals are in *Axminster* and *Bridport*; only the latter now has a minor injury unit (see also *Doctors*).

Axminster Hospital, Chard Street. 01297 630400

Bridport Hospital, Hospital Lane. 01308 422371

Hotels

Over the centuries the fortunes of Lyme Regis's important hotels and inns have changed as much through natural events, as through the fortunes of the town—the George in *Coombe Street*, the original Three Cups at the bottom of *Broad Street*, were both destroyed by fire in the nineteenth century. Some of the present hotels predate the popularity of coastal resorts—The Mariners in *Silver Street*, for instance, was a coaching inn in the 1600s—while as a direct result, entirely new ones have been built—the imposing Bay Hotel on *Marine Parade* was only built in the 1920s. Most of Lyme Regis's larger hotels have bars and restaurants open to non-residents.

The Alexandra Hotel, 4 Pound Street. 01297 442010

The Bay Hotel, Marine Parade. 01297 442059

The Kersbrook Hotel, Pound Road. 01297 442596

The Mariners Hotel, Silver Street. 01297 442753

The Royal Lion Hotel, 60 Broad Street. 01297 445622

Internet

Access to the internet is available at Lyme's public library (for opening hours see *Library*); and also at Lymenet Community Learning Centre, open Monday to Friday and by appointment, where there are a full range of computer facilities.

Lymenet, St Michaels Business Centre, Church Street. 01297 444570 www.lymenet.co.uk

Jazz Festival

This three-day event falls on the first weekend in July and attracts traditional jazz musicians and enthusiasts from all over the country.

Various venues are used for the numerous live acts, from pubs to the *Marine Theatre*, and an umbrella parade takes place on the Saturday morning.

Jurassic Coast

In 2001, the entire run of coast from Orcombe Rocks, Exmouth in the west, to Studland Bay, Swanage in the east, was awarded World Heritage Site status by UNESCO. England's first Natural World Heritage Site, it is now officially protected—and renamed the Jurassic Coast. A nearly continuous 185 million-year sequence of rocks is exposed along the ninety-five miles of coastline, with its unique variety of cliffs and beaches. The official web-site includes a scrolling panorama of the entire coast, and the case study on Lyme Regis has an excellent selection of historic photographs of coastal defence and landslides. (Also see *Geology*).

www.jurassiccoast.com

Landslides

The town has always faced constant natural threat, both from damage to the sea walls by marine erosion, and from the mass movement of the land sloping above them. Although in the past Lyme has suffered terrible damage from storms—*The Cobb* was destroyed completely in the fourteenth century, and extensively damaged in 1824—the problem of landslides became increasingly serious thoughout the twentieth century, with many properties destroyed and several breaches of the sea wall beneath *Marine Parade*. In 1924 there was a major slip of the cliffs at *Black Ven*, and the old *Charmouth* road was lost. Such instability of the land is the reason why the town has never spread west, infilling the large open area of *Langmoor Gardens*, and joining up with *The Cobb* hamlet. There had

been regular failures to the slope behind the massive concrete retaining wall of the gardens, and to adjacent properties, and recently several buildings at *The Cobb* end of *Marine Parade* have been deemed unsafe and boarded up.

Further landslips between Lyme and *Charmouth* have closed sections of the *South West Coast Path* at Timber Hill. In 1997 over ninety boreholes were drilled across the town to monitor the geology and stability of the land. The long-term strategy is now to approach the protection of this coastline preventatively, and to consider the problem not just by way of isolated cases, but broadly and overall, from the cliff tops to the sea-bed up to a kilometre offshore. The most recent phase of works, begun in 2005 and completed in 2007, involved the drilling and installation of over a thousand piles in the area of *Langmoor Gardens* and *Cobb Road*; and new drainage systems to improve the dispersal of water into the sea. A new seawall and jetty was built beneath Lister Gardens; Beacon Rocks at the end of *The Cobb* extended, and the North Wall rocks realigned. The next phase of protection works has been proposed and concentrates on the eastern side of the town at Church Cliff and *East Cliff Beach*.

Langmoor Gardens

This public park and gardens was opened in 1913, having been purchased with a bequest from James Moly of Langmoor Manor, near *Charmouth*. He was an enthusiastic photographer and a pioneer of the Victorian craze for ferns, identifying many hundreds of new varieties. Unmarried, he ended his days as a recluse, leaving his estate for "the educational well being of the inhabitants". The gardens now provide a perfect natural grandstand for views of *The Cobb* and across *Lyme Bay*. Extensive land stabilisation work carried out on the site, and completed in 2007 (see *Landslides*), has enabled a general overhaul of the landscaping,

lighting, and the layout of paths and planting. There is improved access to and from *Marine Parade* below,

and a new woodland walkway at the back to Lister Gardens (named after Joseph Lister, the pioneer of antiseptics, who lived in Lyme) where there is a redesigned mini-golf course, and the former tea-rooms Cliff Cottage. At the *Cobb Road* the commemorative '*John Fowles* Path' continues down to *The Cobb*.

Laundry

Open from 8am to 8pm daily, and equipped with washers and dryers.

Lyme Laundrette, Pooles Court, Lym Close. 01297 445807

Lepers' Well Garden

Formerly known as the Fountain Garden, this small garden is reached by a footbridge over the *River Lym* from the path or 'Lynch' that runs from Mill Green to the *Town Mill*. The re-naming is not accurate—the 'well' is in fact a spring, once thought to have curative properties, and although there was a medieval lepers' hospital in the town, it was situated some distance away in *Broad Street*.

Library

Lyme's small public library is situated near the bottom of *Silver Street* and opens all day on Monday, Wednesday and Friday, and in the morning on Tuesday and Saturday. In addition to the lending library, it has a reference section and a good selection of books on local studies.

Lyme Regis Library, Silver Street. 01297 443151

Lifeboat Station

The present Lifeboat Station at *The Cobb* began service in 1997, and with its three-man crew, the 24-foot 'Pearl of Dorset' lifeboat is launched into the harbour by tractor; the time from alert to leaving the harbour mouth averaging around seven minutes. Over the years several buildings have housed the lifeboat, which was originally kept in a yard on the site of the Cobb Arms until the mid-nineteenth century. The first proper boathouse now houses the public toilets by the bowling green. A larger building opened

in 1884 (now The Slipway shop on the corner, opposite the present station) until the local service was disbanded in 1932; call-outs covered by boats from Weymouth and Exmouth. From 1937 until 1964 the Royal Air Force operated launches from the present *Marine Centre*, but the need for a local RNLI station became clear with the increase of recreational boating in *Lyme Bay*. After a local support campaign, the volunteer service began in summer 1967. The RNLI shop is open from Easter to December.

Lyme Regis Lifeboat Station, The Cobb. 01297 442230

Lifeboat Week

The annual fundraising week for the RNLI, held in the last week of July, includes a variety of attractions both on the water and through-out the town. The most popular event is the usual visit from the Red Arrows aerial display team, who perform in the skies over *Lyme Bay* watched by a huge audience in *Langmoor Gardens* and on *The Cobb*.

River Lym

The River Lym (or 'Lim') rises from springs at the heads of several valleys just three miles north of its mouth at *Gun Cliff* in the town, where it is also known as the Buddle. Its passage is fast, draining the small, steep-sided coombes. Over the centuries, advantage has been taken of the power of the water flow, it

is thought there were once over ten working watermills along its course. The activities of the mills ranged from grinding wheat and barley, to crushing seed for oil and powering looms for weaving cloth, including silk. The old packhorse route along the river to *Uplyme* passes several examples (the free leaflet 'Explore the Lym' describes the

walk—about two hours, there and back); while at the restored and working *Town Mill*, grain is again milled for flour, and there is an exhibition about the river and the work of its mills.

Lyme Bay

The extensive waters of Lyme Bay have been fished for centuries by the communities that line its curving coastline from Torbay in the west to Portland in the east (see diagram on opposite page). It is home to many species of fish (see *Fishing, Sea*), as well as to a variety of crustaceans including crabs and lobsters; while visiting marine mammals can sometimes be spotted on the surface, such as basking sharks, dolphins, pilot whales and porpoises. During the fourteenth to sixteenth centuries, trade was at its peak from *The Cobb*, and the waters would have been busy with boats sailing to and fro between the coast and the Mediterranean, Africa and America. Unable to deal with larger vessels, shallow ports such as Lyme suffered a decline in the later seventeenth century, and for the next hundred or so years *Smuggling* flourished along the immediate stretch of coast, the waters heavily patrolled by excise men. Since the growth of Lyme as a seaside resort during the nineteenth century, the beaches and the bay have gained a new recreational purpose, and nowadays, as well as enabling a diversity of water sports such as sailing and wind-surfing, the clear waters and the many underwater reefs and wrecks along the coast make Lyme Bay popular for scuba-diving (see *Diving*).

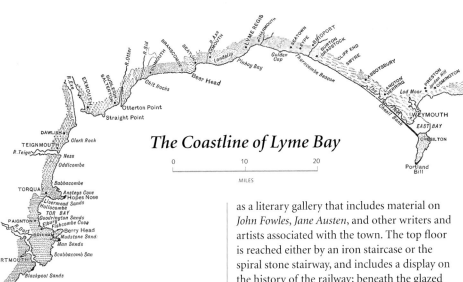

The Coastline of Lyme Bay

0   10   20

MILES

Lyme Regis Museum

Formerly known as the Philpot Museum after its originator, the building dates from 1901, and was built by George Vialls, who had also been the architect for alterations to *The Guildhall* opposite. Thomas Philpot had been

a town mayor and a nephew of the famous Philpot sisters: see *Silver Street*. The museum opened in 1922 with an assembly of material illustrating the human and natural history of Lyme Regis. Major refurbishments took place during the 1990s—as well as necessary remedial work throughout the building, the previously open arches were glazed to make a new entrance and shop, and behind the shop a new glass-walled extension was added, allowing views to the sea. The present layout has displays of Lyme's early and maritime history on the ground floor; the first floor has collections of geology, fossils, and natural history, as well as a literary gallery that includes material on *John Fowles, Jane Austen*, and other writers and artists associated with the town. The top floor is reached either by an iron staircase or the spiral stone stairway, and includes a display on the history of the railway; beneath the glazed cupola, the rotunda gallery has a changing programme of exhibitions. In recent years the museum has won several prestigious awards, but its continual achievement is in presenting the variety of its subjects as an integrated whole, so that the unity of the building is somehow equivalent to the physical unity of the town itself.

Lyme Regis Museum, Bridge Street. 01297 443370
www.lymeregismuseum.co.uk

Marine Aquarium

The Lyme Regis Marine Aquarium & Cobb History is housed amongst the eighteenth-century warehouses at the end of *The Cobb*. Begun in 1958 this small museum has aquarium displays of marine creatures from *Lyme Bay*, alongside objects and

artefacts from Lyme's traditional activities of fishing, boatbulding and sailmaking. By the entrance, a board dated 1879 lists rates of excise for a variety of imported goods.

Marine Aquarium, The Cobb. 01297 444230

Marine Parade

Formerly known simply as The Walk, the elevated sea front runs from *Cobb Gate*, below *Bell Cliff* at the town end, to the bonded warehouses at *The Cobb*, and has, with their sea views, some of Lyme's most desirable, and unstable, residences (see *Landslides*). Beneath the promenade is *Cart Road*, literally the route for goods between *The Cobb* and the town. Although dating mainly from the nineteenth century, the houses vary considerably in style. There are brick seaside villas; the row of

thatched Madeira Cottages; Argyle House (originally an indoor baths); Library Cottage (now two houses, but built as a single-story Marine Circulating Library—the ornate leadwork is French and was added in the twentieth century); and perhaps the most unique, Sundial Cottage, a four-storey Arts & Crafts-style building dating from 1903. Beyond the 1920s Bay Hotel, beneath *Langmoor Gardens*, the twentieth century frontage with its massive concrete walling and shelters is rigorously utilitarian, despite its surface decoration; and a scheme is currently underway to regenerate the structure. At *The Cobb* end, the row of buildings to the seaward side, now mainly cafés and pubs, were developed in the mid-eighteenth century, while the solid stone-built row opposite were bonded stores for the port. The final house on the corner, now a fishmonger, was the Coastguard watch-house.

Marine Theatre

Overlooking the sea, and originally built as Davie's Baths in the early 1800s, Lyme's theatre is the venue for a variety of musical and theatrical performances throughout the year. Productions are staged by the local *Community Players* and *Operatic Society* and by touring

companies. There are regular concerts by visiting rock, pop and jazz musicians, as well

as local fund-raising talent shows and discos. The venue also hosts craft and collectors' fairs. For news of coming events see the publicity display beneath *Bell Cliff*, and the local press.

Marine Theatre, Church Street. 01297 442394

Marshwood Vale

This area of unspoilt countryside north of *Morecombelake* and the coastal hills is the valley of the River Char and its streams, draining the line of uplands south of Broadwindsor and west of the River Brit. Against the backdrop of surrounding hills, the hedgerow-lined lanes and small fields are ideal for exploring on foot or by cycle.

Monmouth Beach

Stretching west from *The Cobb* to Devonshire Head and Seven Rock Point, the beach was the landing point for the Duke of Monmouth and his fleet after sailing from Holland in 1685 (see *The Monmouth Rebellion*). After the failure of the rebellion, twelve supporters native to Lyme were

hanged on the beach. In the nineteenth century the fallen blocks of Blue Lias limestone were used to make hydraulic cement, and a factory and a railway line were built. Remains of the iron track that ran along the beach to *The Cobb*—the 'Donkey Line'—can still be seen at low tide. Later the cliffs were blasted to extract more material, but the introduction of Portland cement eventually ended this local industry, as well as the dust and sulphurous smoke produced by the lime kilns. Production ended in 1914, and the factory was demolished in 1936. Nowadays, the beach is good for fossil-hunting, especially Ammonites (see *Fossils*).

The Monmouth Rebellion

The events of the 1685 Protestant rebellion against the throne of James II began at Lyme Regis. The Duke of Monmouth sailed from Holland with three ships and 82 men, landing just west of *The Cobb* on 11th June. Planning to centre his attack from Taunton in Somerset, he rallied local support, and four days later moved north to *Axminster*—Lyme was then occupied by the Royal Navy to cut off the supply and escape route. Gathering troops on his route north, he made for Bristol with a rebel army of six to seven thousand men. The force was repelled by the King's troops and county militia, eventually suffering a heavy defeat at the Battle of Sedgemoor on the Somerset Levels. Monmouth retreated to the coast to find a way across to France, but he was captured, and beheaded at the Tower on 15th July. In the autumn, the Bloody Assizes swept through the towns of the West country, and reprisals against the rebels were harsh and brutal—twelve men were hung on 12th September near the spot where Monmouth had landed, and their heads and quartered remains were displayed about the town.

Monmouth Street

Connecting *Coombe Street* with *Church Street*, one side of Monmouth Street is now the

Memorial Garden of *George's Square*. It is so-named because it is thought that the Duke of Monmouth stayed at Monmouth House in 1685, with his headquarters at the George Inn, which then occupied the Square, where he ran

his recruitment drive before marching north (see *The Monmouth Rebellion*).

Morcombelake

Two miles east of *Charmouth* on the A35, this small village looks seaward to *Golden Cap* and *Stonebarrow Hill*, and north to the *Marshwood Vale*. It has been home, since 1880, to the makers of the traditional Dorset Knob, a crisp, hand-moulded biscuit ('knob'—means 'hill'). The bakery can be visited Monday to Friday year-round, while the shop sells a range of speciality biscuits, all baked on the premises.

Moore's Biscuit Bakery, Morcombelake. 01297 489253

Museums

There are four excellent and unique museums in Lyme Regis, all open daily in the summer months, and more limitedly at other times of the year. *Lyme Regis Museum* tells the story of the town and its landscape; the *Marine Aquarium*, on *The Cobb*, includes living exhibits from Lyme Bay; *Dinosaurland* has displays of fossils and palaeontology; and the *Town Mill* is a working watermill, presenting a history of mills and milling.

Music and Concerts

There are occasional concerts at the *Marine Theatre* and regular live music at the Nag's Head (see *Public Houses*). The Lyme Regis *Town Band* give weekly evening concerts in summer, from the shelter by the clock on *Marine Parade*. Also see the entry for the July *Jazz Festival*.

Musical Societies

The Lyme Regis Operatic Society was founded in the 1920s, and mounts a new production annually. The Lyme Regis Community Players was set up in 1999 to work on a millennium event for the town; since then they have staged regular productions of plays and musicals. Involvement ranges from singing and acting, to the many background roles of set design and construction, costume, make-up, lighting and stage management (see *Clubs & Societies*). Both companies perform their productions at the *Marine Theatre*.

Newspapers

Lyme Regis News is published from *Bridport* every Friday; and Pullman's Weekly News, published in *Axminster* on Wednesdays, includes a regular section on Lyme Regis.

Parks & Gardens

See the entries for *Langmoor Gardens*; *Leper's Well Garden*; *The Town Mill* (The Miller's Garden); and also *Recreation Grounds*.

Post Office

Located near the top of *Broad Street*, Lyme's post office keeps a wide range of stationery, as well as operating a bureau de change for the conversion of Euros and other currencies.

Lyme Regis Post Office, 37 Broad Street. 01297 442836

Beatrix Potter

The famous children's author visited Lyme in April 1904 and stayed in *Silver Street*. She had already published five of her small illustrated books and was thinking, it seems, about 'The Tale of Little Pig Robinson' (1930) at the time of

her stay—"Stymouth is a pretty little town, situated at the mouth of the river Pigsty… The town itself seems to be sliding downhill in a basin of hills, all slipping seaward into Stymouth harbour, which is surrounded by quays and the

outer breakwater." She made drawings of scenes around the town, and there is a display of material at the *Lyme Regis Museum*. Several of the illustrations in the book are recognisably based on *Broad Street*.

Pound Street

With its broad seaward views, some of Lyme's larger and most auspicious residences have been sited on Pound Street. From the junction

of *Broad Street* and *Silver Street*, the road rises westward in the direction of *Axmouth* and *Seaton*. Just beyond the entrance to *Langmoor Gardens* is the Alexandra Hotel, like many, a former private residence turned hotel; and further along is Stile Lane, the old route down to *The Cobb*, now a pathway to Lister Gardens. At the corner of *Cobb Road* is Belmont, with its distinctive decoration, from the 1780s (see *Elinor Coade*). Leaving the town behind, amongst the villas and bungalows of the Sidmouth Road and just before the junction with Ware Lane, is Umbrella Cottage, a thatched curiosity from the early nineteenth century, with its recently cloned extension.

Power Boats

The Lyme Regis Power Boat Club, based next to the *Lifeboat Station* at *Monmouth Beach*, organises several weekend competitions each year for local teams (see *Clubs & Societies*).

Public Houses

A police report from 1909 states that there was one pub for every ninety-one residents, and recommended the closure of five of them. Along the length of *Coombe Street* at that time there were eight pubs, and of these two were shut down. Nowadays, Lyme has a choice of ten pubs—three of these at *The Cobb*. Most serve food at lunchtime and in the evenings, and both the Volunteer and the Pilot Boat in the town, and the Harbour Inn and the Royal Standard at *The Cobb*, offer varied menus.

The Angel Inn, Mill Green. 01297 443267

Cobb Arms, Marine Parade. 01297 443242

Nag's Head, Silver Street. 01297 442312

The Pilot Boat Inn, Bridge Street. 01297 443157

Rock Point Inn, Broad Street. 01297 443153

The Royal Lion Hotel, 60 Broad Street. 01297 445622

The Royal Standard, 25 Marine Parade. 01297 442637

The Ship Inn, Coombe Street. 01297 443681

The Volunteer, Broad Street. 01297 442214

Railways

With Lyme's growing popularity as a seaside town during the nineteenth century, a scheme to bring a railway line to the resort was sure to arise. However, it wasn't until 1899 that a successful plan was launched—a proposal in the 1840s linking Bridgwater with Lyme Regis, the Somerset and Dorset railway, had come to nothing. The Axminster & Lyme Regis Light Railway opened in August 1903, enabling travellers on the main London–Exeter line to change at *Axminster* for the twenty-minute journey to the coast. Later, some high season timetables during the 1950s and early 1960s ran through coaches direct from Waterloo.

The winding route through the East Devon countryside between the Axe and the *Lym* was very picturesque, with steep gradients and the impressive *Cannington Viaduct*, but the sharp descent to the town left the station half a mile from the sea front, and 250-feet above sea level. Throughout its service there were an average of ten trains a day until the line was closed in 1965, the victim of both bus routes and cars. The site of the station, on the north side of the roundabout on the *Uplyme* road, is now occupied by workshops and a builder's yard, and the former Victoria Hotel the station pub.

Recreation Grounds

Anning Road Playing Fields, by Lym Close west of *Church Street*, is a level recreational area with a football pitch and a children's play area.

Regatta Week

Regatta and Carnival Week is held during mid-August; the boating activities culminate with a carnival parade and a firework display from the North Wall at *The Cobb* (see *Sailing*).

Restaurants

Lyme has a wide range of licensed restaurants serving many styles of food. During the season most open for lunch as well as in the evening. It is advisable to check beforehand both for opening times, and the availability of tables.

Antonio Trattoria, 7 Church Street. 01297 442352

Bell Cliff Restaurant, 5–6 Broad Street. 01297 442459

Broad Street Restaurant, 57–58 Broad Street. 01297 445792

By The Bay, Marine Parade. 01297 442668

Cobby's, 29 Marine Parade. 01297 442699

Hix Oyster & Fish House, Lister Gardens, Cobb Road.

The Harbour Inn, 23 Marine Parade. 01297 442299

Jurassic Seafood Wine Bar, 47a Silver Street. 01297 444345

Lal Qilla, 61 Broad Street. 01297 442505

Lyme Bay Kitchen, 44–45 Coombe Street. 01297 445371

Mad Hatters, 34 Broad Street. 01297 443247

The Millside Restaurant, 1 Mill Lane. 01297 445999

Pizza & Steak House, 2 Drakes Way. 01297 444788

Rumours, 14–15 Monmouth Street. 01297 444740

The Smuggler Restaurant, 30 Broad Street. 01297 442795

The Town Mill Bistro, Town Mill, Mill Lane. 01297 445757

Rock Pools

At low tide most of Lyme's beaches have broad ledges of residual rock, exposing excellent opportunities for rock-pooling (see *Beaches* and *Tide Times*). Anenomes, barnacles, small crabs, limpets, shrimps and winkles are all to be found in the shallow pools left by the tide. It should be kept in mind that these small environments are fragile; and care should be taken on the often slippery, fissured rocks.

Rousdon

See entry for *Combpyne & Rousdon*.

Sailing

Sailing in *Lyme Bay* has become increasingly popular in recent years. Begun in 1921 and formerly based at Victoria Pier on *The Cobb*, the Lyme Regis Sailing Club has a new dinghy park and clubhouse by the harbour and organises many racing events throughout the year (See *Regatta Week, Clubs & Societies*).

www.lymeregissailingclub.co.uk

Seaton

See entry for *Axmouth & Seaton*.

Seatown

Just over three miles east along the coast from *Charmouth*, the beach at Seatown is at the end of Sea Hill Lane, off the A35 at the attractive village of Chideock. Sheltered by the imposing cliffs of *Golden Cap*, Seatown is very popular in summer; the last building, the Anchor Inn, is just a stone's throw from the beach and a well-known stopoff for walkers on the *South West Coast Path*.

Self Catering

Many properties in Lyme Regis and the surrounding area are available to let either privately, or through letting agencies. They range from apartments and cottages, to some of the larger sea-front houses. The main local agent is Lyme Bay Holidays, who produce an illustrated catalogue detailing over two hundred properties; contacts are also available from the Tourist Information Centre.

Lyme Bay Holidays, Wessex House, Uplyme Road. 01297 443363 www.lymebayholidays.co.uk
Tourist Information Centre, Guildhall Cottage, Church Street. 01297 442138 lyme.tic@westdorset-dc.gov.uk

---

Sherborne Lane

Descending steeply from the top of *Broad Street* to the river at Mill Green and *Coombe Street*, this old packhorse route dates back to Saxon times and remains passable to pedestrians only. It was named when Lyme was the property of the diocese of Sherborne Abbey, and the activities of the early settlement were mainly fishing, and the production of salt. Now it contains as colourful and interesting a variety of buildings as any street in

the town—from rows of thatched cottages with neat front gardens, to tall Georgian houses with fine overhanging casement windows.

The Siege of Lyme Regis

In 1644, two years into the Civil War, Lyme was besieged by the Royalist forces then dominating most of the West country. The town defended itself from cannon and musket attacks behind a rampart line enclosing the landward side, with the Parliamentary navy sending supplies and reinforcements from the sea. Skilled leadership and the passionate fighting spirit of both the population and the militia held the garrison firm for two months, despite the King's men bombarding the town from the surrounding high ground. With the build-up of naval ships in the bay and the rumour of the arrival of a landward relief force of the Parliamentary army, the Royalists withdrew, having suffered heavy losses, despite commanding *The Cobb* (which was beyond the town defences) and inflicting great damage by fire to the town's many thatched buildings. The reputation gained by Lyme as a staunchly anti-Catholic stronghold led to the pattern of events of *The Monmouth Rebellion* forty years later.

Silver Street

Common in many West country towns, this street name derives from 'silva' meaning 'wood'. From the top of *Broad Street* it forks in the direction of *Uplyme* and *Axminster*, and would once have been a route through wooded country.

The spire of the Roman Catholic church rises high above the town on the western side (see *Churches*). The Mariners Hotel opposite the junction with Pound Road was the residence of the three Philpot sisters. Like many people, they moved to Lyme in the early 1800s, to pursue building their collection of fossils; its importance was such that it now forms part of the Oxford University collection. Further along the *Uplyme* road, beyond the roundabout, was the site of Lyme Regis railway station, closed with the *Axminster* branch line in 1965 (see *Railways*).

Smuggling

This illicit activity, with its culture of informers and bribery, reached its height in the late eighteenth and early nineteenth centuries; Lyme Regis sits centrally along this notorious stretch of coast, between Beer in the west and Burton Bradstock in the east. Officers of the Revenue Service used *The Cobb* as a base for patrolling the waters, sailing cutters armed with cannon; they also watched from the cliff-top paths on horseback. Contraband goods, such as tobacco and brandy, would be carried from French ports and left in the shallows, before being safely brought ashore.

South West Coast Path

Britian's longest National Trail passes through Lyme Regis—at Ware Cliffs to the west and

Timber Hill to the east. The 630-mile walking route begins at Minehead in Somerset and proceeds west along the coast of the Bristol Channel and the north coast of Devon and Cornwall and around Land's End, and then east along the south coast to Studland Bay and Poole Harbour in Dorset.

www.swcp.org.uk

Spanish Armada

The Armada was first sighted on the evening of 29th July 1588, and fire beacons were lit along the heights of the Channel coast (see the entry for *Ware*, the location of Lyme's warning signal). The first skirmishes with the English fleet, under Drake's command, took place in *Lyme Bay*, including two ships from Lyme: the 'Jacob' and the 'Revenge'. During the days that followed, a stream of small vessels sailed out from Lyme Regis, *Charmouth* and *Bridport*, reinforcing the English fleet with volunteers, supplies and ammunition, while crowds watched the eastward progress of the vast force from the cliff-tops.

St George's, Bermuda

The isolated Atlantic island of Bermuda was 'discovered' in 1609 by Admiral Sir George Somers, who was born in Lyme in 1554. Sailing for Virginia, he became shipwrecked on the island after being caught in a storm. However, Bermuda had been discovered and named already—a hundred years before—by a Spaniard, Juan Bermondez. Somers died in Bermuda a year later; his heart was buried on the island, and his body was returned to England. The towns of St George's and Lyme Regis were officially twinned in 1996.

Stonebarrow Hill

The former route from *Charmouth* to *Morecombelake* along Stonebarrow Lane, just after the road crossing of the River Char, now leads to an area of spectacular coastal landscape owned by the National Trust, a mix of heathland and pasture-land with fine seaward views. The extensive network of paths connects with the *South West Coast Path*, and eastwards to the deserted village of St. Gabriel's and the wooded country behind *Golden Cap*.

Street Markets

There is a market in *Axminster* on Thursdays; *Bridport* on Wednesdays and Saturdays; and on Mondays in *Charmouth* during summer.

Surfing

The waves in *Lyme Bay* are not as favourable as on the north coasts of Devon and Cornwall;

however, beyond the sheltering effect of *The Cobb*, the beaches provide opportunites for both body-boarding and wind-surfing.

Swimming

The sea is excellent for swimming in the summer months and the water clean and safe. The depth increases gently on all the beaches, while at low tide the rock ledges are exposed (see *Beaches*). During the season the sheltered sandy beach east of *The Cobb* is recommended for younger swimmers and paddlers. The nearest public swimming pool is in *Axminster*, which also has a hydrotherapy pool.

Flamingo Pool, Lyme Road, Axminster. 01297 35800

Take-Away Food

As well as traditional English seaside food (see *Fish & Chip Shops*), some restaurants offer a take-away service, including Indian food (Lal Qilla) and pizza (Pizza & Steak House—see *Restaurants* listings). Also see *Bakers* and *Cafés*.

Hong Kong Chinese Hot Food Centre, 15 Church Street. 01297 445182
Mulberry Manor, 10a Broad Street. 01297 444613
Sandwich Bar, 8 Bridge Street. 01297 442728

Taxis

To avoid delays, it is usually advisable to book well in advance for evenings and weekends.

Lyme Regis Taxis. 07900 698569
Matt's Cabs. 01297 442222
Rios Taxis. 07976 779407

Tennis

The nearest public tennis courts are in *Uplyme*, bookable at the post office during shop hours.

Uplyme Post Office & Stores, Uplyme. 01297 443288

Tide Times

Tide timetables for Lyme Regis and Portland are published annually in a small booklet,

readily available in the town. Daily times are also posted at *Charmouth* beach and outside the Harbourmaster's Office at *The Cobb*.

Toilets

Public toilets are situated at the bottom of *Broad Street*, facing the small car park; and in the *Monmouth Beach*, Holmbush, Hill Road and Charmouth Road car parks. There are also conveniences near the centre of *Marine Parade* and next to the Cobb Arms pub. A men's urinal is situated at the end of Victoria Pier, *The Cobb*.

Town Band

The local silver band performs at fêtes and events throughout the year, and gives evening concerts on *Marine Parade* during the summer months. (See *Clubs & Societies*)

Town Crier

The office of town crier is currently held by Philip Street, National Champion in 2003.

The Town Mill

In 1991 the District Council announced plans to demolish part of this derelict, historic watermill and to redevelop the site. The subsequent proposal, by the Town Mill Trust volunteer group, to restore the mill to working condition, is a model of industrial restoration lasting ten years. Records indicate that there was probably a mill on this site in 1280—and the Domesday Book records a mill in Lyme in 1086. The mill was owned by the town and the water turned the mill wheels for centuries, until the addition of steam-power in the second half of the nineteenth century. Commercial milling ended in the 1920s, and for some years the mill was used by the council as a depot. The restoration work involved  extensive archaeological surveys of the site and resulted in the provision of galleries, workshops and a café. With the completion of the three floors of the mill building—the sack floor, the

28

stone floor and the meal floor—grain was once again milled in May 2001, and the buildings made open to the public. The triangular Miller's Garden has also been restored; the planting is based on a seventeenth-century selection of flowers, vegetables, and herbs.

In 2007 the mill began to produce 'green' electricity from the *River Lym*, via a hydro-electric turbine; some of the power generated is used directly in the mill buildings and the remainder sold into the National Grid.

Town Mill, Mill Lane, off Coombe Street. 01297 443579
www.townmill.org.uk

The Undercliff

The eight-mile stretch of coastal path between Lyme Regis and *Axmouth* passes through an unspoilt woodland landscape, classified since 1959 as a National Nature Reserve. The route can only be accessed from either end—there are no landward connecting paths—and the way is almost wholly through dense, ancient woods, with only a few areas of more open scrubland. The isolation of this unique place is a result of centuries of landslips, most famously the Dowlands slippage of Christmas 1839, when acres of cultivated fields and hedges dropped away from the cliff-top. During the following year the spectacular sight became a popular attraction, and extraordinarily, that August the wheatfields were harvested, watched by a huge audience. There are displays detailing the landscape and habitat of the Undercliff at the *Lyme Regis Museum*.

Uplyme

The parish boundary between Lyme Regis and Uplyme also marks the county border of Dorset and Devon. Uplyme is an extensive parish of nearly six square miles, encompassing the high ground above the valleys of the several streams

which feed the *River Lym*. Early settlements in the area are indicated by pre-historic finds at Shapwick Hill in the west, and by a Roman villa at Holcombe, sited on an earlier Iron Age settlement. As Lyme was given to Sherborne Abbey in Saxon times, so Uplyme was given to Glastonbury Abbey, until the dissolution of the monasteries reverted ownership to the Crown, and subsequently to private landowning families. Cloth mills on the *River Lym*, from medieval times to the nineteenth century, made use of the local high quality dyed wool. The Lyme Regis pack-horse route passed through the village; this was the main overland route between the coast and Bristol. It was considered safer to transport goods by land than to navigate the Cornish coast and its pirates. Nowadays, where once there were blacksmiths and shoe-makers, butchers and bakers, the village has just the Post Office Stores, a petrol station, and one pub; locals travel

either to Lyme Regis, *Axminster* or further afield for day-to-day provisions.

Vets

The veterinary practice has a weekday surgery and a twenty-four hour emergency service.

Haydon Veterinary, 59 Silver Street. 01297 442577

Walking & Hiking

"A place is at least as much what may be seen from it, as what it might look like."—Anon. As well the picturesque urban rambles of Lyme itself, the immediate country beyond the town and along the coast offers excellent and varied walking, including sections of the *South West Coast Path*; or back along the small valleys of the streams north of the town; or further inland to the old countryside of the *Marshwood Vale* with its winding lanes and footpaths. The

East Devon Way passes west to east through *Uplyme*, connecting with the Monarch's Way at Monkton Wyld, north of *Charmouth*. The Ordnance Survey 1:25000 Lyme Regis & Bridport sheet (Explorer 116) is the best guide for an overview of the local landscape, and its network of roads and lanes, bridleways and footpaths.

Ware

Ware is situated above and to the west of Lyme, inside the Devon border, on the slopes at the start of *The Undercliff* walk. Nowadays the name is extant primarily in Ware House, and Ware Cliffs—an area of open meadow land to the west of *Cobb Road*, preserved by the

National Trust. This high, open land was an important Armada look-out point and later when a French invasion was feared the warning beacon sited here, when lit, would have started the chain from the coast north to Trinity Hill, near *Axminster*, and west to *Rousdon*, in the direction of *Seaton*. With vigilance, the entire country to the north coast could be alerted in half-an-hour, thanks to the well worked-out network of sight-lines joining hilltop to hilltop.

Laurence Whistler

A resident of *Silver Street* for nearly thirty years, and the brother of the illustrator Rex Whistler. In the 1930s he revived the art of diamond-point engraving on glass, working with both domestic blown glass, such as bowls and goblets, and on larger-scale commemorative window glass. His own compositions tend towards a romantic, sometimes melancholy interpretation of the landscape of Wessex. He published several collections of poetry, as well as 'Initials in the Heart' (1964), the story of his marriage to the actress Jill Furse, and 'Image on the Glass' (1975), a philosophy of his practice and a catalogue of the engraving. He died in 1978—a display in the *Lyme Regis Museum* illustrates examples of his work.

ACKNOWLEDGEMENTS
Several works have proved invaluable in compiling the historical entries in this guide: *A Short History of Lyme Regis*, by John Fowles (Wimborne, 1991), is an acute study of the subject, and highly recommended both for the lucidity of its detail and the fine selection of illustrations. The *Lyme Regis, Uplyme and Charmouth Companion*, by Sheila Bird (Lyme Regis, n.d.) and *The Book of the Cobb*, by Nigel J. Clarke (Charmouth, 1982), are both good general guides. The series of guided walks *Signs of History* (2nd edition, Lyme Regis, 2002), is full of excellent 'on-the-ground' facts. Finally, the *Picture of Lyme-Regis and Environs* (Lyme Regis, 1817, reprint 1985), is an historical curiosity, referred to by John Fowles in his foreword as Lyme's "first tourist guide", and "…a tiny vignette of a long-ago Lyme; and of a long-ago mentality, also". In addition to these publications, Lyme Regis Museum is an exemplary resource, its displays and artefacts offering a rich vein of material, unique both in its particularity and in its diversity.

Information was kindly provided by Mike Lewis, Town Clerk of Lyme Regis Town Council; Geoff Davies, Project Leader, Lyme Regis Environmental Improvements; and Mike Poupard, Harbourmaster and Mike Higgs, Deputy Harbourmaster at The Cobb.

First published 2004
Second revised edition © 2008
ISBN 978 0 9537048 7 3
Typeset in Minion and Syntax
Printed by Axminster Printing Company

Colin Sackett, *Book design & publishing*
7 Hillhead Terrace, Axminster, Devon EX13 5JL
www.colinsackett.co.uk

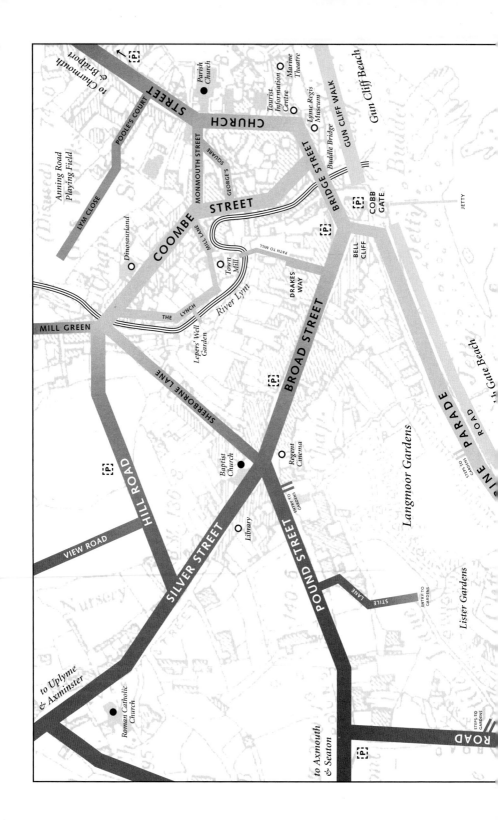